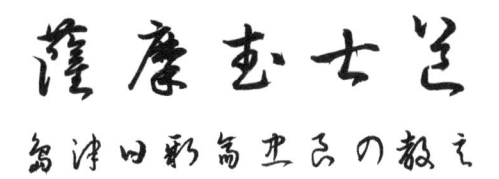

Satsuma Bushido:

Life Lessons by Shimazu Jisshinsai Tadayoshi

薩摩武士道

島津日新斎忠良の教え

Translated by Joe Swift

Satsuma Bushido: Life Lessons from Shimazu Jisshinsai Tadayoshi

Copyright: Charles Joseph Swift 2018

All rights reserved. No part of this book may be reproduced without the express permission of the copyright holder.

Photographs

All photographs contained within this publication are from the personal collection of the author unless otherwise stated. No photographs may be reproduced in either printed or electronic format without the prior written permission of the author.

Published by Bujutsu Translations

Printed by Lulu Press
www.lulu.com

Tokyo 2018

ISBN: 978-0-359-04689-8

Disclaimer

The author of this book is not responsible in any manner whatsoever for any injury that may result from practicing the techniques and/or instructions given herein. Since physical activities described may be too strenuous in nature for some readers to engage in safely, it is essential that a physician be consulted prior to training.

Table of Contents

Author's Introduction..5
Chapter 1: Shimazu Jisshinsai Tadayoshi........................7
Chapter 2: The *Iroha* of Jisshin.....................................9
Chapter 3: The Original *Iroha*.....................................19
Chapter 4: Village Based Education in Satsuma...........21
Chapter 5: The "Other" *Jigen-ryu*................................25
About the Translator...31

Author's Introduction

As a *Karate* practitioner, I feel it is my responsibility to understand the unabridged history of my art, if only to temper my own practices, to make sure they are as close to the original intent as possible.

Eventually, with enough deep study, even the average *Karate* historian will be confronted with an idea that does not sit well with the mainstream party line of *Karate's* origins. In addition to the obvious Chinese influence, there is a deep connection to mainland Japanese culture and battlefield arts.

The main influence would have to be Satsuma, the subjugators of Ryukyu in 1609. With a plausible yet conservative estimate of half a century, the de-facto warrior class of Ryukyu was already actively pursuing Satsuma martial arts. By "de-facto warrior class," we mean those members of the *Pechin* class who were conscripted into a kind of self-defense force. Of course, not all *Pechin* were militarized, but those who were could be considered as the warriors of Ryukyuan society.

After reading the brief chapters in this short presentation, I implore the reader (who I assume would be *Karate* practitioners) to review the various *Karate* philosophies we were all taught back when no one knew what is coming to light these days, as well as the lessons left by Aka Chokushiki to his son[1], to see that the

---
[1] All readers are **strongly** encouraged to read *Okinawan Samurai* by Andreas Quast with Motobu Naoki, the grandson of Motobu Choki and a prolific *Karate* blogger. This book is available globally via Amazon, ISBN 978-1985331037.

mainland Japanese influence on the martial artists of Ryukyu predates the cooption of *Karate* by the militaristic *Gendai Budo* world of 1930-1940s Japan by at least three centuries.

What lies herein is not a direct translation of the poems themselves but based on how the poems are interpreted and used in Satsuma education. Many primary sources, including interviews with top *Nodachi Jigen-ryu* teachers, have been consulted, so I believe the interpretations herein capture the essence of the meaning.

So, without further ado, I invite you to spend the next half-hour or so to read this brief presentation, and meditate on the contents. The words by Jisshinsai are not a mere historic curiosity. There is considerable wisdom contained within to guide us through the complexities of living in a world filled with just so much that is can sometimes be overwhelming.

Joe Swift
September 18, 2018
Tokyo, Japan

Chapter 1
Shimazu Jisshinsai Tadayoshi

Before we look at the translation of this ancient set of teachings, we should take a brief look at its author, his lineage and his legacy.

Shimazu Tadayoshi was born in 1492, and was the tenth head of the Isaku clan, as well as the third head of the Soshu Shimazu family. At the age of three, his father (Isaku Yoshihisa) died, leaving his mother Tokiwa to raise him along with his grandfather Shimazu Hisayasu, who was killed in battle when Tadayoshi was eight years old. After that, his mother married into the Soshu Shimazu clan via Shimazu Yukihisa. This meant that he was to become the heir to two separate clans.

This "soap opera" type of background seems to have been rather common in feudal Japan. In a further plot twist, his son Torajumaru was adopted into the main line of the Shimazu family in around 1526 or 1527, at the behest of Shimazu Katsuhisa. This led to internal strife amongst the various factions in the Shimazu clan, which by 1739, Tadayoshi's side won, driving opposition out of the Satsuma domain.

Tadayoshi later took on the name Jisshinsai, studying Zen, Confucianism and classical Japanese poetry under monks named Shunden and Shunyu, both of whom were in turn students of Keian Genju (1427-1508), a famous priest who visited Beijing on a mission, translated classical Chinese texts to Japanese and taught neo-Confucianism at his own school in Kagoshima. Tadayoshi is also rumored to have learned directly under Keian as a child.

In 1545, he wrote a kind of *Iroha* poem (see Chapter 3), and shared it with Konoe Taneie, a court noble who held the position of chief advisor to the Emperor. Based on this, his new version of the *Iroha* gained favor with the elite of Kyoto, and would go on to become the basis for local *Samurai* education in Satsuma during the Edo Era.

He had four grandsons, who he praised as thus: Yoshihisa the Leader, Yoshihiro the Valliant, Toshihisa the Planner and Iehisa the Tactician. These men carried on his legacy and his teachings became the basis for the local *Samurai* educational system during the Edo Era.

Tadayoshi died in 1568, at the ripe old age of 77, which was considered ancient during that era, at his residence in Kaseda Castle in present day Kagoshima.

Figure 1: A likeness of Shimazu Tadayoshi[2]

---

[2] Image courtesy of the *Kyushu Rekishi Shiryokan* (Museum of Kyushu History).s

Chapter 2
The *Iroha* of Jisshinsai

い　大のことをきゝてもならへても　わがおひにせずばかひなし

No matter how many times you listen to the wonderful teachings of yore, or how many times you repeat these teachings, they have no meaning if you do not put them into practice in your daily life.

ろ　楼のこもはにふの小屋も住む人の　心にこそはたかきいやしき

It doesn't matter if you live in a two-story manor or in a ramshackle hut, the place of dwelling has nothing to do with their actual value. It is the heart of the person living there that determines if they are to be respected or reviled.

は　偲なくも明日の名を扨むかな　今日も今日もと学びをばせで

There are those who make excuses such as being busy today, or not feeling good today to procrastinate in their important academic study, waiting instead for tomorrow to come.

に　いたるこそ友としよけれ我らば　弥ます人おとなしき人

It is easy to make friends with people similar to yourself, but because that does not necessarily create benefits for you, it is better to befriend someone who is better at academic studies or other skills than yourself, and an unassuming quiet person at that.

9

The Buddhas and Gods do not exist outside, but within the hearts of each individual. If you perform evil deeds, you should not worry about what others will think, but you should feel shame within your own heart. The Gods of Heaven and Earth know all.

Just because you may not feel that you are skillful in any particular area, you should not easily give up and throw in the towel. After all, don't they say that even dust, when accumulated and piled up, can become a mountain?

Even when punishing someone whose crimes are so great they call for the death penalty, you should not take the act of punishing them lightly. The sword that brings death and the sword that brings life both reside within the same heart of the liege lord. Careful consideration is needed to avoid any errors in this regard.

Obtaining knowledge or skills will not be a burden nor will they get in your way. On the contrary, the general public respects people who do so, and are ashamed of their own ineptitude in such matters.

り　ほもはも立たぬ世ぞとてひきやすき　心の門の防人にまかすな

Even if the world is in such chaos that logic nor laws prevail, you should not simply do what you want to do merely based on the human tendency to gravitate toward that which is easy rather than that which is right.

ぬ　ぬす人はよそより入ると思ふかや　耳目の門に戸ざよくせよ

You may think that robbers steal in from the outside, but the most frightening thief is that one which sneaks in through your ears and eyes, confuses the mind and steals the soul. You should always take care to lock the ears and eyes, as they are the doors to the heart/mind.

る　るゐすと共人や君が物ほり　はじめて分ける心もちぞよき

Even if it is a story you have heard a million times before, whenever a person of high status or your liege lord is speaking, you should listen with the attitude that it is the first time to hear it.

を　小まの糸が無案に弾かれてや　つとむる道をうしと見るらん

Your own ill-advised deeds will become bad habits, and you will come to think of your duties as too much of a nuisance and begin to disregard them.

わ　れを捨てて君にし向はねば　うらみも起こり迷惑もあり

Unless you relinquish your own private mind and give your whole being to serve your liege lord, then anytime something happens irritation ensues and you will start to complain

Of course, while academic study must also be carried out in the morning and in the afternoon, but the night is especially quiet and suitable for such studies.

It is a good idea to polish yourself by observing the good and bad in other people.

If you do not merely follow your own personal desires, which are the seeds of evil deeds, then your name will not be sullied in the public view.

Does courtesy to people mean to show courtesy (only) to other people? No, it means that courtesy is returned to yourself. Does looking down on other people mean that you only belittle that individual? No, as a result you are only belittling yourself.

They say that there are two times that a subordinate will bad mouth their master. One is when they are criticizing out of a genuine concern for their master, and the other is empty complaining. However, in either case, most of the time what they are saying is good for the master to hear, so the master should listen gratefully.

つ　つらしとて恨みかへすな　されんに恨ひ恨ひてはてしなき事ぞ

Just because you feel hardship at having been done wrong by another person, you should not return resentment. After all, there will be no end to mutual resentment and revenge.

ね　ねがはずば捨てもあらじ　いつはりの事にまことある伊勢の神垣

Even in a world plagued by lies and deceit, the Great Goddess of Ise (i.e. the Japanese Sun Goddess, Amaterasu Ohkami) looks at everything fairly. As long as humans don't overstep our bounds in what we ask of the Goddess of Ise, she will never show favoritism toward one person over another.

な　名を世に残しおきける人も人いもいほかおとらん

Even those who have left their great name in the pages of history were mere humans just like us. They had human hearts just like us. We are in no way inferior to them.

ら　楽も苦も時すぎぬれば跡もなし世に残る名をただ思ふべし

No matter if you are having fun or if you are suffering, those things are mere fleeting instants, and through the passage of time, they disappear without a trace. People should just do their utmost to leave a good name for themselves amongst future generations.

む　昔より忠ならずして残る者のその為にしあはざるはなし

From ancient times, those who do not travel the correct path and become bigheaded cannot escape heaven's punishment.

う　憂かりける今の身こそは先の身と思へば今ぞ後の身ならん

If we understand that any hardships we have in this life are nothing more than our comeuppance from a previous life, then we know that our deeds in this life will be reflected in the next.

ゐ　亥に臥して寅には起くと夕暮の　身を徒にあらせじがため

It has been said from long ago that those who succeed in their academic studies tend to go to sleep at the hour of the boar (10:00 PM) and awake at the hour of the tiger (4:00 AM). This is so that they do not waste precious, ephemeral time.

の　逃るまじきをかねて思ひ切れ　時におりて惜しかるべし

If you find yourself in a situation from which you cannot escape, you should steel yourself to sacrifice your life. With this resolution, you will have no regrets, allowing your heart to remain clear.

お　思はえず迷うものなり身のその　気をはなれて道を守れ

If you are plagued by personal desires, you will unwittingly fall off the path of humanity. You should get rid of all personal desire and live by the right path.

く　美しくとすぐ道をゆけ九曲折の　末は鞍馬の逆さまの暗ぞ

No matter how hard it is, you must stay on the straight path and do the right thing at all times. If you begin to walk down a winding path and become insecure, you will end up falling upside down off the dark path of Mt. Kurama (a famous mountain near Kyoto).

や　やはらぐと怒るをいはば弓と筆　常に二つの翼とをもて

Putting people at ease and getting angry at them can be compared to a bow and a brush, or the two wings of a bird. One without the other is useless.

ま　万能も一心とありし古に　及ばし拙むな器量骨柄

There is a maxim that says one must give their full attention to whatever they do. It does not matter how many skills you achieve, if your heart is not correct, they will amount to nothing. In order to serve someone, you should not merely rest on your laurels. You must learn to think and persevere.

け　賢不肖もちひ捨つると云ふ人も　必ずならば殊勝なるべし

If a person says they will perform politics by using wise people to their fullest and avoiding fools, and is actually ably to do just that, it would be a very admirable thing indeed.

ふ　寡勢とて敵を侮る事もなれ　多勢を見ても怯るべからず

Just because there are few enemies, do not become complacent. Just because there are many enemies, do not become fearful.

こ　こころ軍する者の常なれ　揺ゆれば生き撓はねば死す

The heart is truly the lifeblood of those who do war. If the hearts of allies are as one you will win, if not, you will lose.

When mourning the dead, you must not distinguish between allies and enemies. It does not matter if you recite a Buddhist sutra or not, you should be sincere in your memorial.

Of course, those who are your enemies are detestable, but if you think about it from another angle, they also help you to remain on guard, stimulate you and help you polish yourself. You should regard your enemy as your teacher and sharpen yourself.

If your eyes are blinded and you become lost in this world, how will you deal with the dark path that comes after death?

There are times when rice wine will taste bad like stagnant water, and other times when you will appreciate even river water as much as rice wine. A true leader, even is speaking only a single word, must strive to make those words full of compassion.

Everything you see and hear can, depending on your state of mind, lead you astray or make you achieve enlightenment.

ゆ　ろをはて失ふこともおほるの　いゝ一つの手をば離れず

Capturing the heart of the army, or losing it, depends entirely on the heart of the general.

め　めぐりては糸が方にこそはるーけれ　先祖のまつり孝養の
道

Memorializing your ancestors and staying on the path of piety will come back to you in the end. So, in that regard serving your liege lord is like serving yourself.

み　道にただ身をば捨てむと思ひとれ　かならず天の援けある
べし

Always be prepared to sacrifice yourself in order to do the right thing. With such sincerity, the heavens will listen and you will receive the assistance of the Gods.

し　舌だにも歯の強さをばゐるものを　人はいゝの事からましや
は

Even the tongue knows how frightening a tooth is. Is it really alright for a person not to have the heart to truly see others?

ゑ　酔へる者を醒ましもやらで末に　無明の酒を重ぬるは憂し

In this world devoid of moral principle, it is disappointing that we cannot clear our lost eyes and instead fall deeper into our delusions.

ひ　ひとり者を忘れと思ふ物子に　式にはほすゐあるべし

You should always feel pity for those who are alone, such as elders with no family to take care of them or orphans. You must have a generous, affectionate heart toward your subjects.

も　もろもろの玉やうらのねきは　人に先づよく敎へ習はせ

In all countries (i.e. the feudal provinces of Japan) and villages, the first thing to do is to educate the citizens on the laws and regulations of that place.

せ　善に幼り返れるをば改めよ　義不義は生まれつかぬものなり

If something wrong happens, or a mistake is made, fix it immediately. A sense of righteousness or of injustice are not something you are just born with.

す　少しさをしれりともかれ満ちぬれば　月もほどなき十六夜のそら

You should be content even with just "less than exactly enough." Even the full moon, on 16th night (*Izayoi*) of the lunar month, starts to wane.

Chapter 3
The Original *Iroha*

Jisshinsai chose to leave his teachings in the form of an *Iroha* poem. The original *Iroha* poem dates to the late Heian Period (794-1179), and used each of the phonetic syllabary of the Japanese language exactly once. Due to this, the order in which the syllables are used in the poem has also become of kind of ordering of the syllabary, similar to the "A, B, C" ordering of the alphabet in English and the Romance languages. Indeed, in modern usage, *Iroha* is used to denote the fundamentals of something, such as in English we might say that the fundamentals of a certain field are the ABC's of that field.

In the context of Jisshinsai's lessons, however, the *Iroha* concept is used in a different manner. In this text, the syllables are used as the start of each verse. Thus, rather than being comprised of a total of 47 syllables, it is made up of a total of 47 different verses.

For those with an historical curiosity, the original *Iroha* poem is presented below written in *Hiragana*, *Kanji* and spelled out in Roman letters. An English translation was performed by Professor Abe Ryuichi of Harvard University and can be found online.

いろはにほへと
ちりぬるを
わかよたれそ
つねならむ
うゐのおくやま
けふこえて
あさきゆめみし
ゑひもせす

Iro ha nihoheto
Chirinuru wo
Wa ka yo tare so
Tsune naramu
Uwi no okuyama
Kefu koete
Asaki yume mishi
Wehi mo sesu

Chapter 4
Locally Based Education in Satsuma

The education system of the Satsuma warriors is considered unique in the annals of Japanese history. Known in Japanese as *Goju* (郷中) or *Goju Kyoiku* (郷中教育). It is said to be based on the *Iroha* of Jisshinsai, and the *Nisebanashi Kakushiki Joumoku* (二才咄格式定目) by Niiro Tadamoto (新納忠元). The *Yakumaru Jigen-ryu* sword school was used as the physical basis of the entire system.

It can be likened to a kind of Edo Era Boy Scouts in that the older boys (*Nise*, 二才) are expected to take on leadership roles and guide the younger boys (*Chigo*, 稚児) in various endeavors. Indeed, there is even an unconfirmed urban legend in Japan that Boy Scout founder Robert S.S. Baden-Powell was inspired by the Satsuma educational paradigm when forming his scouts. The age breakdowns of the various classes are as follows.

- *Chigo* is broken into *Ko-chigo* (小稚児) aged 6 or 7 to 10 and *Ose-chigo* (長稚児), aged 11 to 14 or 15.
- *Nise* were aged 14 or 15 to 24 or 25.
- *Osenshi* (長老) were older men who guided the *Nise*, and were those older than 24 or 25.

A translation of the *Nisebanashi Kakushiki Joumoku* is as follows for reference into the mindset of the Satsuma *Samurai*. This is useful when studying the Meiji Era and the mindset of those Satsuma stalwarts who became instrumental in the new government.

- ✓ *The way of the warrior is the first and foremost thing.*

- ✓ The essence of the way of the warrior must be practiced without reservation.
- ✓ If one must join a gathering outside of the group, after the meeting one must return immediately. Do not dilly-dally.
- ✓ It is important to consult and discuss various matters within the group before taken care of them.
- ✓ Protect the old ways, without being ill-mannered toward your peers.
- ✓ If anyone from the group goes elsewhere and finds some points of uncertainty, they should consult with their peers to make sure they do not have any faults in this regard.
- ✓ To not tell a lie is the true meaning of the way of the warrior, and this point must be preserved.
- ✓ The way of piety is not something that should be begrudged. Indeed, it should always be in mind. However, the true essence of the warrior is that he never be caught unaware.
- ✓ Train the body by purposefully walking along roads that lie on hills.
- ✓ A true Nise is not entranced with hairstyles and outward appearances. The first thing in the mind of a Nise must be to remain unaffected and sincere in all things, never straying from the path of piety.

All of the above points must be adhered to strictly. If one does not, then they are not worthy to be called Nise, and the God of War will make sure that their martial fortune runs out quickly.

Other teachings that are said to be common to *Goju Kyoiku* are: do not lose in any endeavor; do not bully the weak; do not brag about any dealings with women, no matter how trivial; monetary and power greed is the most despicable type of desire.

A typical day of *Goju* might look like this:

Time	*Ko-chigo*	*Ose-chigo*	*Nise*
6:00 AM	Learning Four Books, Five Classics, etc. at the home of the *Nise*		Teaching Academics to *Chigo*
8:00 AM	Playing Sumo or other exercise at the horse grounds or shrine yards. Playing educational card games if rainy.		
10:00 AM	Review of morning lessons		*Nise* with posts go to work at the Province office
12:00 PM	*Ose-chigo* teach the *Ko-chigo*		
2:00 PM	Playing physical games (mountain climbing, swimming in the river, tag, etc.)		*Nise* without posts go to study at the Province school
4:00 PM	Martial Arts Training (all)		
6:00 PM	Strictly enforced 6:00 PM curfew	Instructions from *Nise* on how to live as a *Samurai*	Evening discussions on how to live as a *Samurai*, reading, etc.
8:00 PM		Return home by 8:00 PM	

Figure 2: Kaseda Castle from a print made around 1843[3].

---

[3] Image from the *Sangoku Meisho Zue* (三国名勝図会).

Chapter 5
The "Other" *Jigen-ryu*

Jigen-ryu (示現流) was the official sword system of the Satsuma Domain (present day Kagoshima). It was founded by Togo Chui as a combination of the strong points of *Tenshin-sho Jigen-ryu* (天真正自顕流) and *Taisha-ryu* (タイ捨流). It is characterized by its speed and aggressiveness on the battlefield. There were several sub-styles such as the *Ko-Jigen-ryu* (小示現流) of the Ijuin family and the *Ko-Jigen-ryu* (古示現流) of Tanegashima Tokisada.

However, our subject for today is a system known under various names such as *Nodachi Jigen-ryu* (野太刀自顕流), *Yakumaru Jigen-ryu* (薬丸自顕流) and even simply *Yakumaru-ryu* (薬丸流). The simplified histories often refer to this system as a sub-style of the Togo family art, as it was founded by one of his students, but a closer inspection shows that the story is more complex, as it is actually also related to a much older tradition of long-sword practices passed down in the Otomo family during the Heian Era (794-1185).

The technical curriculum of *Nodachi Jigen-ryu* is relatively simple, especially as compared to the Togo school. There are no prefixed *Kata* in the system, and focuses on vigorous solo and paired practice that would be of instant use on the battlefield.

For those who study modern Japanese history may be surprised that most of the stalwarts from Satsuma who were involved in the various skirmishes at the end of the Tokugawa Era were exponents of *Nodachi Jigen-ryu*. This includes such famous people as Arimura Jizaemon (who assassinated Ii Naosuke in the Sakuradamon Incident of 1860), Togo Heihachiro (Admiral of the Imperial Japanese Navy) and

Narahara Shigeru (first Governor of Okinawa Prefecture), among many others.

One story that is a testament to the frightening power of *Nodachi Jigen-ryu* is that of the Namamugi Incident (生麦事件, aka the Richardson Affair). On September 14, 1862, four British merchants, including Charles Lennox Richardson of Shanghai, were travelling by horse through Namamugi village toward Kawasaki when then inadvertently crossed too close to the retinue of the Shimazu regent. Long story short, the Britons, likely out of lack of knowledge of local customs, did not dismount when ordered to, and were attacked by the armed bodyguards.

The initial attack was performed by Narahara Kizaemon, who used the unique *Nuki* maneuver of *Nodachi Jigen-ryu* and slashed Richardson in his left side. Richardson's horse ran several hundred meters as his innards spilled out onto the road. He finally fell from his horse, and crawled toward a local tavern, asking for water. As he was mortally wounded, the order was given to deliver a *coup-de-grace*, and Arimura Nobuyoshi (this is according to oral tradition, but as Richardson's body showed wounds from multiple weapons, we can safely assume more men were also involved) ran over and put Richardson down. Two other men were also gravely injured in the attack, while the only woman in the group was unharmed. This incident led to the Anglo-Satsuma War of 1863. Imagine the steel nerves and sheer skill it must take to slash a man on a panicking horse so deeply that his guts spilled out.

A general outline of the technical syllabus of *Nodachi Jigen-ryu* is as follows.

Tonbo (蜻蛉)
This is the basic fighting posture of *Nodachi Jigen-ryu*, in which the sword is raised high on the right or left side of the body.

Tsuzuke-Uchi (続け打ち)

This is the basic training and technical method of *Nodachi Jigen-ryu*. It can be simply described as striking downward over and over again onto a bundle of wooden sticks (tree branches) lying horizontally across a supporting apparatus.

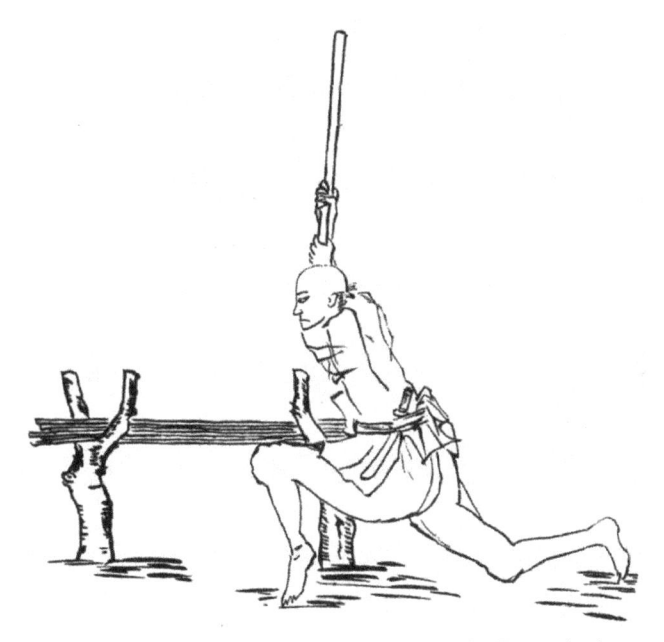

Figure 3. Nodachi Jigen-ryu Basic Practice[4].

Kakari (掛かり)

In this, the second practice, the practitioner runs full bore about 7-8 meters toward the apparatus described above and performs *Tsuzuke-uchi*.

Hayasha (早捨)

This is a two-person practice in which the attacker (*Dashi*) and the defender (*Uchi*) stand several dozen paces away. The attacker uses a long staff whilst the defender uses a wooden

---

[4] This image is found in the *Sanshu Ihou* (三州遺芳).

long-sword. Running toward each other, the attacker performs a side swing at the defender's chest, who leaps in and knocks the staff downward, the performing a right and a left overhead cut. This is not a predetermined exercise and can lead to serious injury.

Nuki (抜き)

This is a method of drawing the long-sword from the scabbard and cutting upward in a single motion. This is the move employed by Narahara Kizaemon in the Namamugi Incident described above. There is a two-person exercise as well as the solo exercise.

Naga-bokuto (長木刀)

This exercise has the attacker swing a long stick downward toward the defender's head, who is in a right-sided *Tonbo* posture. The defender has to strike the attacker's stick downward. Again, this is not a predetermined pattern.

Uchi-Mawari / Uchi-Mawashi (打廻り、打廻し)

In this practice, several dozen sticks are stuck into the ground, and the practitioner does *Kakari* between them, striking them all down as if they were enemies on the battlefield. After all sticks have been struck down, the final test is to perform *Hayasha*, against an attacker who plays the enemy general. There is no set pattern to the number of sticks or the order or method in which they must be struck down. It is indeed a battlefield simulation.

Yari-dome (槍止め)

This is a method of using the long-sword to stop an opponent armed with a spear. Though *Nodachi Jigen-ryu* originally had to rank levels, it is considered one of the secret teachings and is reserved for senior students, taught via word of mouth.

Kodachi (小太刀)

This entails the use of the short sword and is considered a so-called "secret" technique, taught only to the most trusted senior disciples via word of mouth instruction.

Shitsunai no Toho (室内の刀法)

This particular set of teachings revolves around the use of the sword indoors. Due to the pragmatic battlefield nature of *Nodachi Jigen-ryu*, we can assume this set of teachings was developed in the Edo Era or later.

About the Translator

Joe Swift, a native of Van Etten, NY, USA, currently lives and works in Tokyo, Japan. He is a practicing martial artist, as well as an amateur *Karate* historian. He also teaches *Karate* and *Kobudo* in Tokyo. His translations and articles have appeared in several major international martial arts publications and web-based resources. He is a long-time member of the *International Ryukyu Karate Research Society* under Patrick McCarthy, where he has been inducted into the annual honor roll several times for his research and translations. He also serves as the Vice Chairperson of the Board of Directors of the *All Japan Ryukyu Kobudo Federation*, whose goal is to preserve and promote the weaponry skills of Okinawan martial arts.

Selected Translations and Publications
- *Secret Royal Martial Arts of Ryukyu* by Matsuo Kanenori Sakon
- *100 Masters of Okinawan Karate* by Hokama Tetsuhiro
- *Timeline of Karate History* by Hokama Tetsuhiro
- *Okinawan Bojutsu* by Murakami Katsumi
- *Classical Okinawan Goju-ryu Karate-jutsu* by Hokama Tetsuhiro
- *The Essence of Naha-te* by Joe Swift
- *Kobudo: Bojutsu* by Uematsu Yoshiyuki
- *Satsuma Bushido* by Joe Swift
- *The Fall of a Ryukyuan Samurai* by Joe Swift (forthcoming)
- *Itosu Anko: Savior of a Cultural Heritage* by Joe Swift (forthcoming)
- *Karate Kenpo (1933)* by Mutsu Mizuho (forthcoming)